How To Manage Money

Learn The Fundamentals Of Money Management, Zero Based Budgeting, And How To Manage Your Finances

(Recognizing The Fundamentals And Skills Of Personal Finance)

Manual Peters

TABLE OF CONTENT

Money Managing Advice 1

Is Managing Your Finances Vital And Worthwhile? 9

Developing Your Budgeting Method 17

The Advantages Of Good Money Management Skills 40

How To Budget Your Money 49

Planning And Budgeting 74

Budgeting 89

The Best Strategies For Addressing A Budget Deficit 100

Amount In Pocket 117

Kill That Debt 134

Control Your Spending By Following Your Budget. 144

Income: Invest To Increase Earnings 149

Do You Want To Become A Better Money Manager? This Is How: 155

Money Management Apps. 157

Money Managing Advice

If you've ever tried to manage your finances or are currently managing them, it's crucial to understand that it takes more than simply good intentions and individual work. You may effectively manage your funds with the aid of the following advice.

The Key Is Budget:

Budgeting is essential. In actuality, it serves as a road map for your financial operations, making them simple to follow. If you put money in company without a thoroughly thought-out budget, you won't receive anything back in the end. It is like to driving a vehicle without a road map. A precise budget that you will be held responsible to is necessary when your income is constantly increasing. In order to optimize your savings and expenditures, the first money management advice is to create and keep to a budget.

Define Your Relationship with Money:
It's crucial to think about how you feel

about your financial situation. How do you manage your money? What value do you place on your money? What are your money management skills and weaknesses? If you can satisfactorily respond to each of these inquiries, you will be in a position to choose wisely between spending and saving. You must comprehend your connection with money if you want to reach your financial objectives. It will be simple for you to turn your flaws into your strengths after you have defined your connection.

Set Aside a Portion of Your Income: The first deduction from your income is your saving. You will end up with a sizeable sum of money if you set aside a percentage of your income and invest it in an account that pays interest. Your fortune will steadily expand thanks to compound interest, and you will get a sizeable sum as a result. If you put in a lot of effort and are persistent, you can put away a sizable sum of money for a rainy day. Even though it takes a lot of discipline and is not an easy undertaking, if you are devoted, you can manage. Your positive connection with money might lead to savings and discipline in your life. Your activities will be prioritized, and you will control your expenditure appropriately. Before making a purchase, you will be able to clearly separate your necessities from your desires.

Forget on making impulsive purchases; instead, focus on understanding your needs and wants. If you wish to manage your money, you should prioritize your demands by taking care of the most pressing ones first, then focus on delaying the fulfillment of your wants. People often spend their money just because they can. That is most likely the key factor keeping many wage workers in poverty. You can't manage your money if you don't care how your requests are categorized. Spending on the spur of the moment can put you under continual stress. Spending must be determined by your income and the importance of your requirements.

Decide on Short-Term and Long-Term Financial objectives: It's critical to decide on both short-term and long-term financial objectives when you design your budget. It is simple to save money when one works toward a clear objective. You won't be able to save money if your objectives are unclear. For a home loan, for instance, you might choose a 10-year elimination term. In a similar vein, you may use your budget plan to save money for a new house. Budgeting is crucial to sound financial management. Your revenues and expenses are truly included in your budget, together with your short- and long-term objectives.

Avoid using credit: Always strive to save money to pay with cash. In terms of financial advantages like discounts, no additional interest charges, and other perks, cash transactions are much superior than credit transactions. For instance, it's preferable to save for a new entertainment center and purchase it with cash in hand. If you wish to stop paying additional fees Any kind of credit should be avoided.

Create an Emergency Fund: It's critical to save some money for an emergency fund. Your emergency fund will assist you avoid borrowing money when you need it most. Since the future is unpredictable and no one can foresee emergencies, having an emergency fund can help you overcome obstacles with ease. If you don't have an emergency fund and are faced with unforeseen circumstances, your only options will be to depend on credit cards, borrow money from friends or family, or withdraw from your retirement account. You can end yourself in debt and despair as a result of this. You won't have enough money for retirement in the end.

Insurance Protection:

An essential component of protection against unforeseen disasters is insurance coverage. Don't rely only on your possessions; even if you have more of them, you also have more people who are financially reliant on you. Make sure you have the necessary insurance to defend you and your family members against risks.

Health insurance, renter's/homeowner's insurance, life insurance, vehicle insurance, etc. are all examples of insurance coverage. In the event that you become disabled and are unable to work for a while, you have the option of purchasing disability insurance. Insurance is crucial, and you should use this choice if you want to manage your money well. You will be effectively protected from severe losses by it.

Choose the credit card that best meets your needs by comparing available options. Before applying for a credit card, do plenty of research. Compare the yearly fees, interest rates, grace periods, late penalties, and other expenses connected with each credit card. All of these sums add up to substantial financial savings for you.

Purchase a Debit Card:

Debit cards are crucial since they help you remain within your budgetary constraints. You will be forced by a debit card to spend just the amount of money that is permitted in your savings or other bank account. Debit transactions are instantly debited from your checking accounts, and your monthly statement will include all of your transactions in one location. You will be able to quickly follow every dollar thanks to this function. If you are aware of your means and expenditures, you can control your spending in the proper way. Debit cards are a wonderful alternative if you wish to discipline your spending behavior.

Monitor Your Spending:

To stay inside your budget is the final but not the least step. Just creating a budget is not enough. Make sure your spending stays within the allowed range and adjusts as needed as time goes on. An efficient method in this respect is the envelope budgeting technique. Particularly for those with lesser incomes, these budgeting strategies are beneficial. At the end of the month, you may add up your spending using a spreadsheet. You have other choices that may aid in the analysis and modification of your expenditure. The first goal is to keep inside your budget.

the conclusion

Making decisions on how to distribute your wealth in order to increase it in the future is a key component of successful money management. If you are committed and have a clear and planned connection with your money, you may reach your objectives of accumulating the most riches. You need to decide on your immediate and long-term objectives and quit wasting money. Purchase a reliable insurance plan and establish an emergency fund. Keep tabs on your spending and modify as required. Your wealth will grow steadily after you start doing all of these wise behaviors, allowing you to realize your ambitions without worrying about money.

Is Managing Your Finances Vital And Worthwhile?

Let's face it; if you don't believe that managing your finances is necessary or worthwhile, you won't do it. But if you've read this far, I assume you think the topic is important in some way. I can tell you about my own experience with money management, but I can't speak for everyone else.

I hadn't even gotten my first job yet when I was in my late teens and just out of college. But I quickly started working. Making money, paying bills, and then spending the remainder was my money management strategy back then. I think many people may identify with this predicament. However, there were other occasions when I did strive to save every penny but ended up spending it all because I felt cheated out of the enjoyment and contentment. It was a vicious cycle that lasted for a few years until I became engaged in a company and learned a whole different money-management strategy, which unquestionably transformed my life. It was essentially transformed.

I claim to have perfect money management abilities because, among other reasons, doing so makes me very happy and enables me to see daily increases in my fortune. These days, I'm excited about making money and managing it.

Managing your finances allows you independence and may even inspire you. It enables you to manage every facet of your life without having any regrets. It is crucial that you understand how to manage your money and do it effectively if you value independence, wealth, maximizing your earning potential, and enjoying everything that life has to offer.

Following is a list of the key benefits of good money management:

Your ability to make, keep, and grow your money will improve as a result of: - promotes financial freedom and discipline -helps you see where your money is going -financial growth -promotes wealth -encourages you to associate with financially savvy people -allows for freedom and security -your ability to make, keep, and grow your money will increase -gives financial confidence

You will undoubtedly begin to recognize all of these benefits as your ability to handle your money improves, and you will also advance personally. You'll become fired up and enthusiastic about the subject, and you'll also start looking for and figuring out methods to go above your present financial situation.

Section 3. The 3 Ds

Even though it may appear simple, it might be difficult to transition from desiring to doing. This is often because individuals haven't mastered a certain skill, even if it may seem easy to perform. Mastering the three Ds—

decision, discipline, and determination—is one of the finest methods to get from idea to action.

Decision

What exactly does it mean to decide something? To me, it is making a firm decision to carry out a task or accomplish a goal. Making a choice is not a serious matter for everyone, however. Just another thing you say, really. It's crucial to make a serious decision and avoid settling for mediocrity when deciding to manage your finances or develop the habits needed to do so.

I had trouble making judgments, which caused me to spend a lot of time debating my objectives. However, I became aware of this. Your objectives will be easier to reach and you won't have to question if you should do anything every day after you have made a solid choice about what you want to do, how you will do it, and how you will stick to it. Your ability to make a firm choice will be crucial to how quickly and successfully you establish these new habits. It is usually advisable to educate yourself thoroughly on the subject(s) you are interested in as well as determine the specific reason(s) why you desire to do so in order to make judgments more quickly.

Discipline

How disciplined you are will depend on how consistent you are. In addition to choosing to take charge of your money, you need also choose to maintain your discipline.

My father used to yell at us as kids whenever we did anything that was out of place or not in order: "YOU HAVE NO DISCIPLINE." I didn't pause to consider why he said it back then because, to be really honest, I felt it was absurd. Looking back, that really made a lot of sense. He was arguing that we lacked discipline because, despite knowing the proper thing to do and sometimes doing it, we tended to act inappropriately most of the time because we lacked self-control (discipline). Truth be told, developing habits requires discipline since it enables you to repeat actions and thoughts over and over again, which causes things to stick with you forever. In the same way that you never forget the lyrics of the song you love to sing, that nasty habit you can't break, or regular activities like driving, eating, and walking, etc. It's also wise to be aware that developing a habit takes 21 days.

Finding a method to appreciate what you are doing is a smart strategy to maintain discipline. You won't have any trouble performing anything consistently or again if you like it.

Determination

What lengths will you bare? It won't be a one-time activity, a sprint, but a marathon to manage your money. You will sometimes find it difficult to remain composed. People will first tell you it isn't working, and you will initially believe them. In such circumstances, will you be able to maintain your resolve and work your way through the darkness into the light?

I already remarked that it took me a few months to get used to things. There were days when I wanted to give up everything over those months since I was essentially simply travelling back and forth. But I didn't because I had a compelling reason for not doing it—I had a goal to get my finances in order, and I knew that if other people could accomplish it, I could too, maybe even better.

The best suggestion is to create a compelling why, or justification, for your money management objectives if you want to remain committed to them. The reason you need to succeed at something, not simply why you want to. When things become difficult and you begin to doubt your ability, it will support you in staying in the fight. And keep in mind that you don't have to be flawless to succeed; all you need to do is make sure you don't give up.

Developing Your Budgeting Method

Estimating a person's income and spending over a period of time is the practice of budgeting. In other words, it predicts how much money will be made and spent over the course of a certain length of time.

The difference between budgeting and frugal spending is that the latter implies expense reduction, whilst the former may or may not.

While frugal spending does not allocate money to expenses, budgeting does. Finally, whereas frugal spending does not provide a list of costs, budgeting does.

Planning your costs depending on your income is what budgeting is all about. When you have a healthy budget, you spend less than you make in terms of income and you accurately plan both your long-term and short-term spending. Many individuals find this to be an uncomfortable feeling since they feel as if they are denying themselves of items they could really afford. However, it is quite helpful and need to be regarded as a money management strategy.

Financial success depends on having a budget. It is not only for individuals who have little money to spend but also for those who have a lot of money. It enables individuals to decide how best to spend their money so that all of their needs and desires may be readily satisfied. The leftover money is put away for retirement and unforeseen costs.

It's much simpler to prepare for significant costs that you won't be able to cover all at once when you effectively manage your money.

Many people make bad financial decisions.

Financial errors are rather common; in fact, individuals make them all the time. However, once you begin planning, recognizing some typical budgeting errors that others do can help you avoid them:

Don't maintain a record of every spending and purchase. It is far more beneficial to note your overindulgence than to try to forget it. You may now proceed with more caution as a result of this.

Make impulsive buys. Spending a lot of money on unplanned minor purchases is wasteful. Consider how much sweets and gum you impulsively purchase at the supermarket. Over time, everything adds up.

You are miserable because you deny yourself so severely. It might grow annoying after a time, and you might opt to blow the budget simply to make up for the enjoyment you missed.

exceeding planned spending. Shopping is enjoyable, and many individuals find themselves persuaded to spend more money than they intended. Long term costs may result from this error.

Creating a budget

Observe your purchasing patterns.

As in the case of frugal spending, a person must maintain track of their spending patterns for a certain amount of time. On the other hand, budgeting often calls for a month's worth of spending data since it needs deciding which costs will be incurred on a monthly basis.

Make a list of every cost you incur.

Make a record of all the expenditures you have made in a month as you keep tabs on your spending patterns. There should be a balance between required, variable, and one-time costs.

A person's lifestyle would be significantly affected if essential costs were cut since they are intrinsically important to their survival. Among them are costs like food, rent, and recurring obligations like insurance.

large costs that may be decreased without having a large negative effect on a person's life are known as variable expenses. These expenditures include those for consumables, public transit, and electricity and water bills.

Contrarily, casual expenditures are those that may be substantially decreased or eliminated without materially changing a person's lifestyle.

This category include almost all entertainment expenses.

Look at your earnings and outgoings.

Following the creation of a list, a person must assess the income and costs they experience over the course of a month. Knowing whether they are living within, or barely over, their means is critical.

Create a financial strategy.

The revenue and cash put aside to cover the expenditures stated are summarized in a budget. It is an approximate estimate of the amount of money that will be put aside to pay for certain expenses.

Use the leftover money for urgent needs.

A person should observe that after allocating costs, there is still money left after finishing the budget. The discretionary amount is this. Whether or not to utilize the extra cash for an emergency must be decided. This is significant since the individual may always utilize money from the discretionary fund in case of an emergency. However, it must be distributed in accordance with its intended uses. The emergency's goal and purpose must be in line with one another.

attempting to stay as close to the budget as you can.

After developing the budget, it is now time to implement it. A guy should adhere to his spending plan for the next few days. He shouldn't go above his planned amount for a certain item. Because the budget now acts as a guideline for how he should spend his money, it is critical to keep this in mind. Long-term financial problems will arise from failing to stick to the budget.

One of the most effective ways to control income and spending is via budgeting. It also enables him to see how much money he will need to spend over a certain length of time. Even though creating a budget takes work, implementing it and following it might be beneficial in the long term.

Pay attention to your money.

You'll be able to keep tabs on your spending and ensure that you're adhering to your spending plan. You may take action to lower your food costs if you discover that you are overspending in one area, such as food.

To keep track of your money, you'll need a tool you're comfortable using. Here are a few of the most popular budgeting instruments used by experts:

Register and notepad

The simplest tool to utilize is a notepad that you may use to keep track of all your everyday spending. It need to be portable enough for you to carry. By the end of the day, you should move your data into a ledger. Examining your ledger will allow you to evaluate your spending patterns.

Smartphone applications

You may utilize free applications to replace your laptop system if you have a smartphone. Every time you spend money, all you have to do is take out your smartphone and write a record of your spending. It must become ingrained in you each time you make a purchase. This is a better choice than a notebook since we always have our phones with us. In contrast to the notebook, the app does not immediately fill up. Simply remove the program and reinstall it to clear the data if it does start to fill up.

If you don't want to invest money, there are several free applications with constrained capabilities that nonetheless provide similar services. Most individuals can monitor their spending on a daily, weekly, and monthly basis using the features of free applications.

Spreadsheet

You should keep track of all your spending in a spreadsheet-style file rather than a ledger. If you are accustomed to using this kind of instrument, you will be able to make computations and comprehend the data more rapidly.

You may use them if you have Microsoft Excel installed on your PC or Mac. Use open source software that you can get from the Internet if you don't have access to a computer. The characteristics offered by open source options are enough for this purpose.

Budgeting techniques

A budget is a tool that enables you to regularly monitor the money entering and leaving your accounts. We have also spoken about the importance of budgeting and its advantages. We will go through the necessary procedures in this chapter, along with a model budget that you may use as a guide for making your own budget.

assembling and planning

Generally speaking, it is a good idea to figure out how you will create your budget. If you have a strategy in place, creating a monthly budget won't be difficult. Simply choose a time and location, and go there once a month. Make sure it is a quiet area of the home with no outside distractions. You could also want to think about a suitable time, like Saturday morning.

The next step is to collect all the data you'll need to make a budget. You may prepare it manually with paper and a pen if you prefer the traditional method. It is simpler to create a budget using Excel sheets or one of the websites that provide the format, however. Before using it, you must first log in and register.

Formatting

Typically, it makes sense to structure your budget. To plan your budget, you must construct tables and fill them out. The page is often divided into four parts, with the first column carrying the name of the income, the second column containing the amount, the third column containing the name of the cost, and the fourth column containing the amount. This framework will make budget preparation easy and fast for you. It is also a suitable format to use if you have another structure in mind, such as listing all of your income and adding it up, followed by a list of all of your expenses and adding them all up. You are free to use whatever format you like, and if your program or website has one, you are also free to use it.

Revenues

The first item you should include in a budget is your income. Your pay, interest on deposits, passive income, and investment returns are just a few of the ways you might make money each month. The revenue column should include a list of all of them. Review each statement you have access to, including your portfolio, bank account, and pay statement. Include all of your revenue together with the corresponding figures in the income field. The amount of money in your account and the maximum amount you may spend while staying within your budget will depend on your income. Once all of your revenue has been reported, add it all up and put the result in the "total" column. Remember to take one-time income, such bonuses, out of the calculation.

Total

When you have both totals, subtract the greater number from the smaller number. The bigger figure will represent either the overall revenue or the total costs, depending on how much of each item there is. If your total is positive, meaning you have more money than spending, you are in the black, and if your total is negative, meaning you have more costs than income, you are in the red. This suggests that you are overspending, which might have negative effects. If you have extra money, you'll need to decide how much to invest and how to save it.

Adjustment

Making improvements to your budget will ensure that your revenue exceeds your costs. You must alter your spending habits and make an effort to cut down on any needless expenditure to achieve this. Simply go over your spending plan and remove any items that are not at all required for you. Don't panic; you can always add them back whenever you have enough money to comfortably pay off your obligations.

There are several reasons to stay inside your budget.

One of the personal financial laws that everyone who wishes to save money must go by is creating a budget. You may learn how to save money by learning to live within your means. But why is following a budget so important? Although most individuals are aware that maintaining a budget will enable them to save money, there are several additional benefits as well:

so that it will increase in value over time

If you've never created a budget before, you may be apprehensive, but don't be. A budget is not a means of limiting one's lifestyle, as many people believe. The precise opposite is, in fact, true. A budget is the instrument that will enable you to attain financial freedom, which is something you've always desired. When you check your bank account at the end of the month, do you ever wonder where your money goes? You will have more money to spend if you can train yourself to establish reasonable monthly spending.

You must budget money specifically for your objectives.

You must first determine how much money you will have left over after paying your taxes. The next step is to calculate your costs. The "50/30/20" spending plan is a common option. It entails distributing "50%" of after-tax income to pertinent costs including lodging, utilities, and transportation.

With the remaining "30%" of your income, you should focus on long-term objectives like purchasing a house. The remaining "20%" may be allocated to immediate objectives, such a yearly vacation or an emergency fund.

Know how to live comfortably within your means.

What's the most effective approach to begin? Tracking your spending is the first step in determining if you are adhering to the 50/30/20 budget. If not, you must figure out what costs you can cut without affecting your revenue. Use budgeting tools to keep track of your spending for the following 30 days. Now that your monthly payments are paid, you may redistribute your funds. You should also confirm that you are saving money towards your objectives.

in order to avoid debt

You may live within your means and avoid being in over your head in debt by using a budget. You'll be able to stay under your spending limit. In other words, unless you have a plan in place, you won't go into debt. You can prevent debt by creating and following a budget, and you can also pay off debt by doing so.

Create a favorable credit history

The greatest method to get a strong credit history is by adhering to a budget. Make a note of your recurring loan payments and add them to your needed spending. By doing this, you may stay on track with your spending plan and pay off your whole debt at the end of the month. Additionally, it will assist you in avoiding pointless debt and interest fees.

Avoid participating in the "rat race"

Every one of us want to quit working at some time in our lives. This is only possible if we begin setting aside funds for retirement and wait to use them until we are prepared to stop working. Set aside money from your budget for long-term objectives to put in your retirement account in order to make your ambition a reality.

Nobody likes to feel constrained by their spending, but when you are first learning about personal finance, keeping a budget is the best way to keep track of your money. Everybody has a distinct way of life and budget. Personal finance is referred to be "personal" for this reason. As a result, establish your budget on your income, objectives, and needs.

Motivators to keep your spending in check

Even while it might be challenging, it has several advantages, as we said previously.

Managing your finances on a monthly basis provides you a feeling of total control and you in your future planning. No matter what your financial objective is, creating a budget is the first step in achieving it. It will enable you to establish priorities and make an efficient money management strategy.

But it may be harder than it looks to keep to this plan. You may be tempted to buy the newest smartphone with your vacation money. Even if the "I want to" part of your brain can try to convince you otherwise, there are several things you can do to stick to your budget:

Find a someone who will hold you responsible.

Finding someone who is in your circumstance is crucial when settling on a budget. This might be a spouse or relative. Additionally, you and a buddy may update your weekly budget on Facebook. Set objectives, keep track of them, and own up to your errors. If you have support and encouragement, you'll be able to keep on course and concentrated.

Be truthful.

Keep in mind that having some fun will encourage you to stick to your spending plan. It's simple to rebel when you start to feel like you're missing out on something. Make as many reductions as you can without getting rid of anything.

Decide on a day when you won't make any purchases.

When you spend a little bit here and there, you may not believe you are doing much spending. When you sum up all your modest purchases after a month, however, you'll see that you've really saved a ton of money. Don't go to the store every day to pick up stuff you forgot. These frequent travels might cost you a lot of money.

Set aside a day, or maybe three days, without any obligations, to handle it. If you don't have the appropriate components, why not improvise?

The Advantages Of Good Money Management Skills

When it comes to managing money, the advantages of having strong money skills are immeasurable. Effective money management will enable you to pursue new avenues in life that were previously closed off by a lack of funds. Learning how to handle your money will inevitably provide the disposable income needed to have an unrestricted life. Few other "kills" can compete with good money management.

Live a more stress-free lifestyle

When you manage your money properly, you should be able to live a more stress-free life. Money is one of the most stressful things in someone's life, thus it has to be managed properly to lessen the stress associated with it. Effective money management can prevent some of the serious consequences that come with not paying your bills on time, sending your children to college, and any other kind of stress that money brings to one's life. Always having some spare cash on hand can make you feel lot more comfortable. Money's security contributes significantly to assisting individuals in lowering stress.

Realize Your Dreams

Everyone has different life goals. However, almost every dream that a person might have involves money in some kind. Most individuals can only achieve their dreams if they can effectively manage their finances, if they have a financial component at all. Without money, you won't be able to take your child on the vacation of their dreams. That is just not how the world works. However, if you successfully manage your finances, those dream vacations become a lot more attainable.

Money may help you reach all kinds of goals, even those outside of vacations. You could fantasize about sending your child off to college or seeing your favorite professional sports team in action. Chances are that your aspirations will cost you money in any case, and effective money management may be the key to achieving your goals.

More travel and vacations are needed

Even if a dream vacation isn't in your plans, you'll probably agree that you'd want to be able to travel more. Traveling and seeing the world are two things that are quite expensive. For the majority of people, having high financial standing is their only chance of traveling and seeing the globe. There is a reason why the majority of people who have money choose to spend it traveling the globe and seeing all the earth has to offer with their own eyes.

Enjoy the ultimate fantasy

Sadly, in our world, money has an impact on how much freedom a person has in their day-to-day existence. You can essentially do whatever you want if you had unlimited funds. If you have enough money, you can nearly do anything, including sleep in, eat out, go to the moon, and almost anything else. Gaining some excellent money management skills will allow you to continually expand your independence in life.

Money Management: How to Manage Your Finances Effectively and Enhance Your Lifestyle

We all know that handling money, whether it be your personal finances or the cash coming in and going out of a business, can be frustrating and at times quite challenging. Most people struggle, as the term goes, "to make ends meet" as well as to pay their expenses. Most of us just want to be able to manage our finances wisely and work to better our lifestyles.

Home Money Management - Understanding finances and handling your money at home shouldn't be difficult. There is a wealth of information on financial matters available on the internet so that you may organize your finances wisely. Understanding how mortgages and credit work, as well as how to avoid going into debt, are crucial topics to address so that your money doesn't manage you – you need to manage your money! Many websites provide assistance by offering free online budget planners and budget calculators.

Do your homework before using these websites since there may be security issues when entering account information. These websites sometimes contain flaws and miscalculate budgets in addition to being unreliable. The majority of the time, purchasing an online budget planner will provide you access to much superior software that will make it simple for you to handle your personal finances and bank and credit card accounts. Additionally, you will get extensive support and assistance, as well as many other services that the free websites do not provide.

These online budget planners and calculators allow users to see their accounts, run reports on their spending and saving habits, and create clear graphs and pie charts that break down their spending by category so they can understand where their money is going. All of the numerous features that are available will allow users to plan and stay within their budget while staying on top of their day-to-day finances.

Money Management in Business - For every business owner, proper money management should be their first responsibility. The basics are crucial when beginning a new company, such as setting up a business bank account, accounting (DIY or hiring an accountant), and how payments will be accepted, including the conditions of credit. There are many various software options available on the internet to assist with money management, cash flow, budgeting, and accounting if you decide to manage your own finances.

It's crucial to choose the appropriate bundle to meet your unique company demands. The majority of these systems allow users to create invoices, maintain track of accounts payable and receivable as well as any other crucial bank account balances, as well as to keep track of cash flow, which is the movement of money from one place to another.

Selecting the Correct Money Management Software - You must decide which money management solution is best for your needs while selecting one. Do your research before buying software online whether you just want to keep track of your expenses or want to regain control of finances that have gotten out of hand. With the correct software, managing your money can be really simple. You can even plan, budget, and save for a better, debt-free future!

How To Budget Your Money

You don't need a how-to manual on spending, but it wouldn't hurt to get a little guidance from financial professionals. These straightforward spending practices might really enable you to save a few dollars. You need to be careful where you spend every dollar because you are not yet a billionaire. If you want to spend and save money effectively, pay attention to the spending advice provided below.

Knowing your life priorities is the greatest approach to get the most of your money. Rent, transportation, and food are among the top priorities for someone who is paying their expenses, for example. In order to prioritize your monthly debt payments, home costs, and amusement, be sure to take into account all of your spending.

Utilize a system of monetary allowances. Keep an envelope for each of your expenditures, and set aside money for the month.

Choose a credit card with a cash back rewards program when applying for one. The cash return may help you save a lot of money, even if you have to accept a lesser yield for cash back incentives compared to fixed rewards. It resembles receiving a discount on each thing you buy. These little sums do build up to significant amounts over the course of months.

When considering a purchase, keep the following questions in mind: "Will this purchase make my life much easier?", "Will I be happy in the long run if I buy this?" and "Is this a necessity or a wish?This strategy forces you to spend money only on the things that are the most helpful, things that you will use and that will provide you pleasure for a long time.

Despite the fact that there are numerous venues to have fun, for some reason, many of us choose to spend our free time in malls. While I don't think visiting a mall is terrible, it may be costly. And if you want to save money, you must resist the urge to purchase just for enjoyment.

Reduce your impulsive spending as well. You've probably went to a mall a number of times, impulsively purchased a thing after seeing it, and never used it again. Don't squander your hard-earned money in such a way. Set a timer instead. Why does it matter? Simple: Set a time restriction for yourself, say one day, if you feel the temptation to purchase a new appliance, item of clothing, product, or anything else for that matter. Make the buy only if, even after a full day, you still feel that you need or want the thing. When you stop making impulsive purchases, you'll be surprised at how much money you may save at the end of the month.

Work hard, manage your money, and give yourself a reward for your dedication. Make vacation funding a top priority on your list. Your long-term financial stability will be aided by the benefits.

If you pay careful attention, you'll see that a lot of the food you purchase really makes its way into the garbage can rather than onto your plate. Why is it the case? Because most of us tend to refill our refrigerators even when they aren't fully empty. As a consequence, a large portion of your money and food are wasted. Therefore, be careful to utilize all of the ingredients at once rather than regularly reloading your refrigerator. Despite the unusual mixes of the dishes, you will still save a ton of money.

Additionally, have a plan and a list with you the next time you visit the grocery shop! Choose the meals you want to prepare for the whole week and plan your grocery shopping accordingly. You may save time as well as money this way. And if you stop to think about it, time is also money!

Keep a journal where you may record all your purchases. Every thing you buy should be noted, along with the reason why you got it and how it made you feel. Review all of your purchases in this journal two or three weeks later to identify which ones have you second-guessing your decisions. To spend money sensibly in the future, you must cease doing them now.

resisted the want to spend money. This involves several actions. Taking the example of avoiding spending money on a buddy who constantly encourages you to go shopping. Stop browsing internet catalogs on your phone all the time! Your heart will want to purchase if you are looking at clothing or electronics, but your head will know what is best for you and your pocketbook. Therefore, think twice the next time you swipe through catalogs or go out with that buddy of yours.

Last but not least, if you get carried away, don't give up. Since we are all just human, it is typical for us to take time to get acclimated. However, if you work hard and have patience, you can change things. Additionally, even a minor modification to your spending pattern matters since tiny sums quickly compound into larger amounts. Just stay true to your goals and keep your attention on how to resist temptation. Accurately determining what is genuinely essential to you is the key to spending money effectively. Following on from spending patterns, we'll talk about monitoring your money. Turn the page to learn more about the following effective money management tool.

HOW TO BUY

There are several methods for saving money each month.

• A More Recent Approach: Pay Yourself First

Why It Works

The best saving strategy is to take care of yourself first. This implies that you designate a certain portion of your paycheque as your pay (how much), and you pay that money to yourself before paying your expenses or anybody else. This sum may be $25, $100, or even 10% of your paycheque. It may be whatever quantity you like. The crucial component is that you pay yourself first rather than afterwards. Most people pay all of their bills in full first, then set aside any leftover funds. That method of saving doesn't actually work for the majority of people since there is nothing left over to save.

If you pay yourself first, you'll save money since it will now be your first priority. The nice thing about this method is that it drives you to make adjustments elsewhere and your savings continue to grow if your budget is a little tight.

Making your own payment first also makes sense. Why, in any case, are you going to work every day? to generate income for someone else? No way. You go to work to make money for your family and yourself. That is why you should pay yourself first—to ensure that your first priority is taken care of: you. Anyone else is unlikely to take care of you since they presume that you are taking care of yourself.

- Pay yourself automatically

You should establish an automated system for paying yourself first so that you don't even have to think about it; it just happens. You may set up automatic transfers with your bank (either online or at your local branch) or ask your employer to deduct a certain amount and put it in your RRSP.

Most users of this method discover that they very quickly become used to living on a bit less and fast forget the amount that they are paying themselves in their savings account. Amazing things occur automatically when you nearly forget about automated savings and allow them to grow. Automatically saving $25 a week results in a yearly savings of $1,300. Now, if someone followed this consistently throughout a lifetime, they would immediately get some fantastic outcomes. From the time they were 25 until they were 65, if someone automatically saved $100 every paycheque (bi-weekly), they would have about $415,000 if they only received a 6% rate of interest. Of course, after a person's mortgage was paid off, they could afford to save more. Thus, their total sum might end up being substantially bigger. Hopefully, you can see how simple an automated system where you pay yourself first may make it possible to do large things.

- How to Automatically Become a Millionaire

Another incredible benefit of using automated withdrawals or transfers to pay yourself first is that you can utilize it to automatically become a millionaire. This may seem absurd, but it really works. From the time they were 25 until they were 65, if someone had $200 routinely sent from each of their bi-weekly paycheques into their investment account, they would have amassed nearly $1,000,000 if they had averaged a 7% rate of return on their investments. Therefore, a regular person may become wealthy without winning the lottery. This plan is entirely feasible, but it would require a little more sacrifice than most people are ready to do in their twenties.

- The best way to save money is to have a spending plan.

The best way to save money is to create a spending plan or budget (learn how to create a budget). Making a budget allows you to calculate your income and expenses. Once you are aware of these two factors, you may seek for ways to decrease your expenses or raise your income in order to set aside an amount of money that you can afford to save. The largest corporations in the world operate in this manner, as do the majority of successful businesspeople worldwide. This procedure requires some initial effort and a check-up every year or two, but it is effective.

The key to this approach, if you want to call it that, is to identify what you are spending money on so that you may start planning your expenditure. You will gain control over your spending if you start to plan it, and you will then be able to make plans to spend money from your savings. To put it another way, you will prepare to deposit money into your savings account. Many people dislike planning their spending since it requires some effort (once a year). Nobody is predicting easy success, but this little amount of work will pay you big time in many areas of your income. We challenge you to give it a try; what have you got to lose?

• Money Saving Tips: How to Use Them

1 An account for retirement savings

If this is too much for you, start by just depositing your funds into one savings account and growing your savings from there.

You may set aside money on a regular basis for a down payment on a home, a car, or your retirement. All of this money may be put into one account to start things going and can double as an emergency fund as long as you don't have "emergencies" on a regular basis.

- Use several savings accounts

You may open up several savings accounts if you locate a bank or credit union that provides a free savings account. When you are paid, you may then deposit money into each of these accounts for each specific item you are saving for. This will prevent your money from being accidentally wasted and ensure that it is there when you need it.

These accounts don't necessarily have to be actual bank or credit union savings accounts; they might also be high interest accounts, Tax Free Savings Accounts (TFSAs), RRSPs, term deposits, mutual funds, or other assets. Just be careful not to put money into a long-term investment that you may need in the near future (read more about the differences between saving and investing for the long run vs the short term).

- Below Your Mattress

We hope you won't do this. Every thief is aware that this is where to start their search. A roommate is the same. Then there was the one who dug a hole in his backyard and buried $10,000 in cash in a glass jar. He later dug it up and found that the water in the soil around the jar had frozen in the winter, causing the jar to break. Then, water filled the container, turning the money into a soupy mash. Most of the bills were unrecognizable, so he was unable to cash them in. He was only left with one broken jar of pricey soup.

Within Your Safety Deposit Box

Many people do this; just ask the tellers at your bank; they can smell it (old money smells). It is undoubtedly safer to store cash in your safety deposit box than in a mattress or in the backyard, but not much safer. Money kept in a safety deposit box serves no useful purpose. You don't get any interest from it. The government covers the money you put into a bank account up to $100,000 (and there are other ways to acquire more coverage than this), so how can you trust the bank with the items in your safety deposit box if you can't trust it with your money?

- In Your Account

Saving money in a checking or normal savings account is not a good idea. Most of them pay almost any interest at all. This is due to the fact that the bank loans out your money to other people while you aren't using it. Regular bank accounts may be used often or you may need to withdraw money fast, thus a bank cannot lend out that money for an extended period of time since you may need it. The bank earns money when they can lend your money out for longer periods of time and at higher interest rates, therefore when they can do so, you will get more interest.

- Accounts with High Interest

These types of savings accounts are often far more restrictive than standard savings accounts, but they pay much higher interest rates. Check to see whether your bank or credit union is offering you a competitive rate (you can't negotiate, but you can move) before you start saving. These kinds of accounts are often safe, practical, and their interest rates typically increase when bank interest rates do.

Additional Investments

You may use a variety of other assets to preserve your capital, including money market funds, bonds, equities, mutual funds, and so on. It is advisable to invest in something secure if you want to use the money you are saving within five years. A high return savings account or a long-term deposit into a tax-free savings account works just well for the majority of people. These are safe options, and you can be confident that your money will be there when you need it. However, the same cannot be said if you decide to invest in anything that carries a significant amount of risk. similar to the stock market.

• How to Find Money Each Month to Save

Some things are simpler said than done, such as saving money. You want to save money, but where can you get it if you don't currently have any additional funds? Here are some excellent places to look: Where to look for money to save each month.

- Ria working

Put the additional money you start receiving after you receive a raise in the bank. You were living less before. Do you truly need these extra few dollars, or is your savings account in need of them more?

- Reward from work

If you get a bonus, bank that money as well. Because your bonus is extra money that you cannot count on, you do not need it to cover living expenses. This is why it is referred to as a "bonus" to your regular pay. Bonuses are ideal for saving. If you need your income to cover living expenses, you probably have other financial difficulties that need attention first.

- Extra pay from employment

You may volunteer for longer than usual in certain jobs. Consider working a little more each week, then treat your overtime pay as something sacred and save it in a special account.

- Extra large communication

If you get commission for your work, think about setting aside a portion of any very large commission payments. It is so simple to lose money and then have no idea where it went. Use portion of your extra large paychecks to create something you will remember, such as a lovely retirement, a cozy house, or whatever else you would want to save for. Make a lasting retirement plan for yourself by using your money.

Purchase it from the government.

Tax refund.

If you get a tax return, boost your savings with the money. Speak with your tax advisor or a reliable source to learn how to pay less tax so that you may get a refund or qualify for a larger one. Many people may lower their tax obligations by contributing to an RRSP and/or increasing their charitable contributions. These solutions may be simple and affordable if you set up an automated system where your RRSP or charitable donation is automatically deducted from your bank account or withheld from your paycheck.

- Tax Assessment

Make sure your tax assessment value is accurate if property values have declined significantly in your community. Apply for a reinstatement if it is not false. This may save you a ton of money on property taxes in communities where property values have fallen sharply.

- Claim all expenses

If you are self-employed, do your taxes yourself or do they get done for you by a professional accountant who has the credentials CA, CGA, or CMA? If one of these professionals isn't doing your taxes, you might be missing out on significant tax savings. If you believe that these types of accountants are costly, that may be the case, but it is sometimes more costly to pay the government thousands of dollars in unnecessary taxes than to pay a competent accountant a few hundred dollars to identify these savings for you. If you're very frugal, you might try hiring an accountant once to see if you're missing any deductions, and then you could go back to your previous method of filing taxes and use the tax-saving advice you learned from the accountant.

Check Your Expenses for It

- Seek out a cost to reduce and save that money.

There are some people who recommend that you improve your savings by giving up smoking or drinking alcohol. These suggestions are valid, but there are also other significant methods to save money. One approach that many individuals might save money but sometimes overlook is to take a close look at how much they spend on their hobbies. Some individuals spend a lot of money on personal training, protein supplements, golf, skiing, and other sports. They don't even think about how much they spend since they think they are spending it on something worthwhile or something they like. Cutting down on your hobby spending, even if for a little time, may be a wonderful choice to consider if you have an urgent concern like getting out of debt.

Planning And Budgeting

You shift your money around and devote it to your expenditures via budgeting and planning. Budgeting is required for all regular monthly living costs, including those for housing, food, clothes, and transportation as well as insurance. You'll need to figure out how to set up a budget and make spending decisions depending on your income. You may track your money using apps or any other tools that you find most effective. Consider your personality and the system that will work best for you.

Family vacation and holiday spending preparation takes more time than personal money, according to studies conducted in the US and other countries.

A clear road to the goals you and your family are pursuing will be provided through time spent on this venture with goals and objectives. You won't get to the life you desire if you don't know where you want to go. To help you in this crucial period, I've highlighted two methods that you may evaluate and use in your everyday life.

You need a budget (YNAB) is a fantastic software to think about since it is designed for zero-based budgeting. To ensure that you are aware of where every dollar you earn is going, use a zero-based budget. If you make $4,000 per month, (YNAB) will assist you in creating a budget and ensuring that your income and spending are equal.

This way of thinking is based on taking charge of your spending and directing your money where it needs to go. This idea is fantastic, and although it will cost you $50 a year for the service—just over $4 a month—it would be worthwhile to handle your funds at that price. By presenting a student ID, transcripts, or another kind of enrollment documentation, students will be allowed to access the program for free. Non-students may still use the app for 34 days without paying anything, after which they must pay the yearly price.

The Mint app is an additional option. With Mint, you can manage all of your expenses in one location. The software is web-based and contains simple-to-use tracking and budgeting functions. It costs nothing to join up, and adding an account simply takes a few seconds. The main functions of Mint are spending monitoring and budgeting.

After initial setup, budgeting is quite simple. Download the app, link your accounts, and you're ready to go. There is no monthly subscription or price for annual access since Mint earns money by suggesting services to you.

With the help of Mint, you can manage all of your payments, credit cards, bank and savings accounts, and financial institutions in one location. All of your information will be updated and categorized by Mint in one place. Your data will be analyzed by Mint, which will then provide savings recommendations. You'll be able to set up reminders for bills and stay on top of all of your monthly expenses all your credit cards will be found in one place so you can monitor them and track you're spending as well as your balance and card limits. Instead of having to remember the passwords to five or six separate accounts, you can pay your bills, check your money, and do other time-consuming tasks with this app. You'll be able to create reminders and generally save time while planning and budgeting for your own finances. Free to use and a nice software to test.

In conclusion, creating a strategy that works for you and a dress are all you need at this moment. Budgeting and planning are crucial for your financial success. Although You Need A Budget

(YNAB) is just $50 a year, I don't believe I could rationalize paying that when I could develop a system that is extremely comparable to this one without spending that money. On the other side, Mint is a good software to check out; it's FREE, and having all of your accounts connected and accessible in one spot saves a ton of time.

Set spending priorities.

The first things you need to spend time establishing up are your work and earning an income, coupled with your budget. You will have to make purchases at certain points. The choice will be made based on requirements and desires. You will need to give priority to where you will spend your money.

The "Only Investment Guide You'll Ever Need" by Andrew Tobias comes highly recommended. This book won't teach you any revolutionary tactics, but it will offer you a fresh perspective on how to look at product prices and make the most of the resources you do have.

I learned about Tobias's book while browsing the internet when I came across the Millennial Money website's post on "How to Calculate the true cost of anything." Andrew Tobias first published his book in 1978, it goes on to describe that there's no reliable method of speedily accumulating wealth. However, by maintaining the premise that your income should not exceed your expenses as well as being aware of financial advertising that intends to separate you from your money. Becoming financial literate will enable you avoid being targeted as a consumer that others can benefit from and is aware that setting up an emergency fund ins vital and to use a tax-sheltered account for investments. Tobias stresses the long-term costs of living expenditures and the need of avoiding investing money that you will need over the next five years.

This part will concentrate on how you should spend your money based on what you need rather than what you desire. It's crucial to keep that in mind as you start your road to money building. It is quite simple to go out and spend money on things you don't really need, like an updated phone, but if you don't prioritize and concentrate on where your money should go, you're more likely to spend it elsewhere and on things you don't actually need. Never forget that your hard-earned money, whether it comes from your job after taxes or another source, is highly valuable and should only be used sparingly. Americans are thought to earn between $2 million and $10 million on average during their lifetimes. Setting spending priorities will aid in directing your choices and ensuring that the majority of the money you make stays in your wallet. It's not how much money you earn, but how much money you retain, said entrepreneur, real estate investor, and author Robert Kiyosaki.

It's incredibly simple to get into the trap of earning money and spending it on things that you don't really need or that don't benefit you or your family. Making selections will be fast and simple if you refer to your planning and budgets. Your most crucial goals will have been prioritized after you have a strategy and a budget in place. When you get into the trap of overspending, $2 million to $10 million will wind up in someone else's bank account without you even knowing it since you were careless with your spending.

It is advised that you spend 50% or less on your essentials, which include housing, transportation, health care, insurance, staple foods, and clothes, in the book "All Your Worth" by Elizabeth Warren and Amelia Tyagi. The next 20% or more of your income should go into savings, which should go toward retirement funds, bank accounts, and paying off credit card debt. You may spend the remaining 30% or so whatever you choose, perhaps on fine new designer clothing, possibly eating out, family holidays, or anything else you feel like doing.

Richard Jenkins of MSN Money's "The 60% Solution" suggests allocating 60% of your budget to fixed costs like mortgages, car loans, insurance, utilities, and taxes. The remaining 10% should be set aside for unforeseen costs, such as vacations, prescriptions, and maintenance. The remaining 10% should be allocated to long-term savings or debt repayment. This allocation of your funds would cover credit cards, student debts, saving for a vehicle, and paying off your house. The next 10% should only go into retirement accounts, such as Roth IRAs or 401ks. The remaining 10% is your discretionary spending money, so do with it what you like.

Liabilities and Assets

You can make choices more quickly and organize your money if you understand how assets and liabilities vary from one another. When you reach the tipping point that we previously mentioned after accumulating enough assets, you may choose to buy liabilities or follow the desires that were covered in the previous section.

Assets are anything obtained (such as dividend stock, real estate, or intellectual property) that puts money in your pocket for the purposes of this book. You get income from your asset every year, quarter, or month. A liability is something you acquire that deducts money from your bank account. Items include automobiles, yachts, jewels, and anything else that requires post-tax funds.

Gaining an understanding of the distinction between an asset and a liability can help you increase your net worth more quickly and avoid making mistakes that will have long-term financial repercussions. It's not the end of the world if you make a bad decision and spend all of your hard-earned money. Making choices and then reflecting on them is what life is all about. That will be covered in a later section. The point I'm trying to convey here is that spending all of your cash on a liability will have consequences, both short- and long-term. You must determine the amount of time and effort required to get that revenue and contrast it with the cost of the thing you are purchasing. Each individual must evaluate if the time invested in earning the money was worthwhile before accepting the choice that was reached.

The Formula for Success

Most millionaires and billionaires have achieved success by developing and putting into practice a plan. Make a strategy to purchase assets that will need to generate revenue, then use that money and your generated income to purchase further assets. It's a simple strategy, but one that needs commitment and effort over an unanticipated length of time.

An example of an asset is real estate, especially real estate that produces income on a monthly basis. including stocks that pay dividends. shares purchased in a company that will make payments on a yearly, quarterly, or monthly basis. Intellectual property includes things like patents, trademarks, and other created possessions that generate income for the owner in the form of royalties.

Liabilities are landmines in life. You need to watch out that you don't follow in the footsteps of your pals who buy and take on responsibilities.

When liabilities are accumulated, they rob you of your hard-earned money, which is what keeps you alive. Then, you act as a middleman for your money. You get your revenue in exchange for your time, and you promptly transfer it to meet any obligations you have assessed to be necessary or useful to you. Liabilities include debt incurred by using credit cards for purchases or the purchase of a luxury automobile, the value of which will drop 10% as soon as it leaves the dealership lot and further by 10% by the end of the first year.

Therefore, the key is to follow the formula of using earned money to buy assets that generate income, then reinvesting that revenue together with your earned income to buy additional assets. When your income finally outpaces your costs, you will have reached the tipping point and can start investing in assets. This equation is used by the wealthy to grow their fortune and maintain their standard of living.

Once you've reached that tipping point and want to buy liabilities or indulge, another straightforward approach you may use is to buy an asset with the goal of utilizing it to pay for a liability.

You wish to buy a Corvette Stingray, for instance. That brand-new car has a sticker price of $59,999. You calculate the monthly borrowing fees for the car to be $1,131. You can find every premium feature and accessory you may desire in this automobile. Therefore, while shopping for an asset, you should aim for that monthly payout. Look around and find an asset that will generate that much in monthly cashflow. after you have that asset, you may use it to pay for the automobile, and after you've paid it off, you'll have a monthly income-producing asset worth $1,131.

Budgeting

There are two categories of individuals: those who despise regulations and those who like them. If you fit into the latter category, you will simply like the concept of a household budget; if you fall into the former, however, you will find it challenging to fall in love with a budget. The fact is, in order for you to manage your finances, a healthy home budget is a must.

The budget comes first when discussing how to handle the money you currently have since it is a crucial component of financial management. A budget is a written plan that outlines how you will spend or save your money. It enables you to properly manage your life within the constraints of your monthly income and helps you allocate the required amounts of money at the beginning of a financial month. If you still find the notion of a budget unsettling, you will undoubtedly fall head over heels for it once you give it a try. Your budget will significantly improve how you feel about your financial situation.

This chapter focuses on showing you how to create a successful home budget. Some of you may have even attempted budgeting in the past, but it didn't quite work out for you; the reason being that you lacked the budget creation advice you need. You will learn how to create a household budget in a professional manner as well as how to gauge how well you adhere to the spending plan.

You must keep in mind that a budget is not simply for difficult times. A budget is always a good idea. Consistently sticking to your budget ensures that the prosperous times last as long as possible.

How Important a Budget Is

You may not be aware of all the benefits of maintaining a budget since it affects your psychology in addition to merely tracking your income and expenses. Here are five factors that make budgeting crucial and why all financial professionals advise it.

Budgeting Maintains Your Focus: Making a budget keeps you committed to achieving your long-term objectives and assists you in identifying them. How can you ever be able to accomplish your life objectives if you live your life aimlessly and spend your money on every little glittering thing that catches your eye? Budgeting pushes you to create a goal map; this goal map will include sections for saving money, tracking your progress, and realizing your ambitions. Your budget serves as a constant reminder of your long-term objectives, which motivates you to continue working toward them. Here's how it works: When you see an awesome pair of shoes or a brand-new blouse that you want to purchase, you'll stop when you discover that it is out of your price range. It could be painful at first, but once your budget prompts you to remember that you're saving for a new automobile, it'll be simple for you to resist the need to purchase and walk away satisfied.

prevents you from spending money that you don't have: Today, credit card debt is pervasive. Numerous spenders have racked up credit card debt as a result of their penchant for blowing money they don't even have. In actuality, the average credit card debt in the US was $6,194 in 2019, and this number is steadily rising. The fact that 55% of Americans who use credit cards also owe money on them shows how common and simple it is to spend above your means.

Before credit cards, customers could easily see whether their expenditure was within their budget. If they had enough money at the end of a month to pay the rent and save some, they would know they were on the right road. Everyone utilizes credit cards nowadays, and they have no clue if they are financially stable or not; the only time they go deeply in debt do they become aware that anything is wrong. But if you make a budget and adhere to it, you'll never find yourself in such a precarious situation. You will know precisely how much should go toward savings, spending, and income.

Yes, calculating numbers and keeping a budget journal are not as enjoyable as going on a buying spree. Imagine instead that you will be flying off to Turks and Caicos for your vacation rather than scheduling a debt counseling session for the next year.

A Successful Retired Life: A budget not only prevents you from squandering money and ensures that you spend wisely to avoid debt, but it also makes sure that your savings are on track. You will undoubtedly benefit from this little additional effort in the long run if you set aside a portion of your monthly income for savings in your budget.

assists you Recognize the Errors: Did you find it challenging to recall the last time you spent money incorrectly? If you were good with money, you would have known the answer straight immediately. By creating a budget, you may thoroughly examine your spending habits. You'll realize that you're squandering money on pointless expenses. Do you fully use the data allotted on your pricey mobile data plan? Are new PS4s really necessary? With a budget, you may evaluate your spending patterns and make changes in line with your objectives.

Making a budget reduces stress: Keeping to your spending plan can also help you sleep better. Many of us have spent many sleepless hours worrying about our bills and rent. Without a budget, you let your finances rule your life. Regain control over your life, accept responsibility for it, and you'll feel more at peace.

How Do You Create A Budget?

For creating a household budget, there are three key tenets.

Make a comparison between your present monthly income and expenses.

Reduce your expenditure to stay inside the parameters set by your income.

Spend your money wisely by dividing it among the several needs.

You were instructed to pose a series of questions to yourself in the very first chapter. If you had provided answers to those questions, you would have been prepared to create your budget; nevertheless, if you haven't done so yet, don't worry. We'll try it again, and this time, you need pay attention to the directions if you want to create a budget. It is advised that you go through this chapter in its entirety before creating your budget.

Find yourself a fair budget template before you begin reading and writing. It is completely up to you whether you like to budget on paper or using a computer or smartphone. While the latter is simple and practical, many individuals still prefer the earlier way. You may immediately begin entering the data after downloading an example budget template online.

Gather any recent financial records you can locate in step 1. You want as much material as you can get your hands on. Every bank statement, pay stub, utility bill, supermarket receipt, and other document containing information about your income or spending from the previous six months should be available. Finding the average monthly income and spending is the key to making a successful budget, thus the more data you can gather, the more accurate the monthly average you come up with.

Step 2: Identify all of your revenue sources. Make careful to keep track of all of your revenue sources if you are self-employed or have more than one. When creating your budget, use your lowest monthly income from the previous year as a minimum income amount if your income is changeable (varies depending on the volume of your company or sales). If the income comes in the form of a regular paycheck, when taxes are deducted automatically, you may merely utilize the net income since it will be sufficient. Add up all of your revenue from the previous six months, then divide that total by six to get your average monthly take-home pay.

Step 3: Compile a list of all your costs. It won't be simple to locate all of your payments that were documented in paperwork. Only by keeping track of every dollar you spend and adding it all up at the end of the month is it possible to determine exactly how much you spend each month. What then, when we lack all of that information, can we do? Write down any costs you can think of that you already know the amount of. These might include the mortgage payment, auto insurance, tuition for your children, etc. Using historical receipts or an informed guess as to how much will be spent, you might estimate the amounts for which you lack information. For the first month, you would have to do this, but after that, you would have everything recorded.

Income vs. Expenditure in Step 4. You are in excellent standing if the findings indicate that your revenue exceeds your outgoings. This also implies that you may direct the extra money toward certain goals, like debt repayment or retirement savings.

Furthermore, you might think about using the "50-30-20" budget if your income exceeds your outgoings. In a 50-30-20 budget, your requirements or necessities should get 50% of your income, your desires should receive 30%, and your savings or debt repayment should receive 20%. On the other hand, you'll need to make modifications if your spending are higher than your income.

Step 5: Make the necessary adjustments. Your ultimate objective should be to have the income and expenditures at the same level if you were successful in precisely identifying and cataloging all of your costs. When your costs exceed your income, look for areas where you might reduce your spending. You can reduce almost all of your variable costs in some way. Since most of these costs are not necessities, it is simple to save a few dollars in each category to get closer to balancing your income and spending.

The budget's creation process ends with step 5. The idea must then be practically carried out as the following step. Monitoring and documenting the amount spent in each expenditure category once the budget has been established is a critical step, and you should do this every day. To keep track of all these costs, use the same spreadsheet that you used to build the budget.

You may avoid overspending by estimating how much money you spent in each area over the course of a month. This will also help you uncover any unneeded or problematic spending patterns. Instead of submitting all the costs for the month at once, you will find it far more convenient to set aside a little amount of time each day to record your spending.

Use the envelope approach if you're hesitant to use this kind of budgeting. Here, money is divided into distinct envelopes for different categories, and only one envelope's worth of money is used for any given reason. You'll have to stop making purchases in one category whenever the money in that envelope runs out.

The Best Strategies For Addressing A Budget Deficit

The word "budget deficit" is most often associated with governmental budgets, but it may also refer to a hole in your own budget. Simply explained, a family budget deficit occurs when spending total more than income. A budget deficit may have a number of causes, but there are two main groups. either a decline in income from factors like unemployment or sluggish company, or a rise in costs from things like unforeseen expenses or accidents. Whatever the reason for a budget shortfall may be, there are budgeting techniques you may utilize to achieve a budget surplus.

Reduce expenses

The most obvious choice is definitely this one. You need to make an effort to cut down on your spending when you have more money going out than coming in. If you are experiencing a short-term financial shortfall, cutting spending could be more difficult. The rationale behind this is that all major expenses like rent and electricity bills are fixed and won't vary significantly soon. However, there is a lot of room in the typical budget to cut costs. Try to reduce your food costs by 20%; it could be difficult but it's not impossible. Additionally, refrain from saving money in the short term for luxury items or non-essentials like trips or furnishings.

Eliminate any planned savings, such as vacation and retirement savings, and adhere to a strict budget in order to reduce your budget deficit. If you can live without it, attempt to put off purchasing anything despite your best efforts to resist the urge.

RISE IN COMMISSION

Although it isn't the simplest option, this is the second most apparent solution to close your financial gap. Almost everyone can reduce spending, but not everyone can boost income, particularly those who hold down full-time employment with regular salaries and are unable to perform a side gig. There are several strategies to enhance our income; we'll go into more depth about them in the next chapter.

BE PREPARED FOR THE DEFICIT

If you know that a large payment is coming up and that you could have a budget shortfall, you can start making plans to close the hole. Starting to save money before there is a deficit is a great idea. For instance, if you anticipate that your monthly costs would be $500 or more than your monthly income, you may plan for a 6-month parental leave by setting up $3000 before taking time off from work.

AVOID MAKING IT CASUAL

Budget shortfalls are very typical, and practically everyone encounters them sometimes throughout life. However, if you see that your budget deficit continues to be an issue, regardless of whether you are working or not or if you are in any special circumstances, you undoubtedly have a problem. You may still apply the aforementioned tactics if your expenses consistently outweigh your income, but you'll need to go to the next level. You need to cut the fixed expenditures as well, not only focus on lowering the variable expenses like groceries money. Sell your vehicle and switch to public transportation, or look for a less expensive housing. Your long-term financial shortfall won't be resolved by asking for a raise; instead, you should look for a higher-paying position.

Maintaining the Plan

Though it is the most rewarding activity, sticking to your budget and keeping consistency is not at all simple. Maintaining a budget doesn't need you to deny yourself of all the finer things in life. As long as it remains within the parameters of how much you may spend, you can still continue to do the things you like, such as hosting family dinners once a week or renting new movies.

Even if you spent a lot of time and effort creating a well-thought-out budget, the hardest part is sticking to your plan. Even if you've used up all of the entertainment money, you may want to steal a few dollars from your vacation funds to buy your kids a new Xbox game. Although your emotions might be persuading, your willpower will be crucial. Here's how to keep on track even when you feel powerless in the face of your spending urges.

A buddy for accountability: The game is won via teamwork. You will have a very difficult time following through on your goals as you are a one-man army. When it comes to household expenses, having someone on your side is quite beneficial. The majority of us can make our spouse our accountability partner. However, it may be anybody, from a relative to a work colleague. You may proceed as long as your perspectives on money are compatible. Following your budget plan becomes much simpler when you have someone to prevent you from straying from your financial objectives and to motivate you when you're lacking in inspiration.

Avoid outright getting rid of your credit card, but cease carrying it with you when you go shopping. A credit card will never assist you stay to your financial plan; it can only serve to divert you. Keep this in mind and internalize it. Use just the money you have if you wish to stick to your strategy. Never utilize borrowed money with high interest rates that you don't own. Use just the cash or debit card that you have instead.

Be Realistic: By establishing unattainable and unworkable norms, you just set yourself up to break them in the end. Making sure your budget is reasonable is crucial. First of all, you won't be able to adhere to the strategy as soon as you begin if you set completely unattainable targets. Second, if you create a budget that is really challenging to stick to, you will eventually stray from it. Both times, you break the plan, which leaves room for more budget infractions. Examples of absurd budget solutions include eliminating all of your entertainment spending or drastically reducing your shopping budget to the point that you only eat bread and beans for dinner every night. You are more prone to revolt against the budget if you deprive yourself. Cut back rationally, but don't eliminate everything you love.

Use the Envelope System: One excellent technique to reduce budgeting errors is to use envelopes to separate your money into the several categories. We often mix up the numbers while managing and moving them about on spreadsheets or budget worksheets, which may be annoying for many individuals.

However, separating your cash into envelopes for each area of spending is a great approach to prevent the confusion of numbers. Additionally, it provides budgeting a tangible sense and prevents you from blindly taking money from one area to spend in another.

OPTIONS FOR INSURANCE

One of those dull subjects that few people truly comprehend is insurance. Usually, after spending five seconds attempting to learn about it, you either fall asleep or get a migraine. So let's dispel some commonly held myths about insurance as well as some basic insurance guidelines.

There are many different sorts of insurance, each with a distinct function and an endless range of alternatives. Let's start by discussing the insurance coverages that several states already mandate you have, making it possibly criminal to "go without." With the enactment of recent legislation, health insurance is now required on a federal basis. This indicates that having it is often required in order to avoid paying penalties. Whether you agree with this or not, it is still generally a good idea to have some kind of health insurance. It's always a good idea to at least have coverage that can handle such catastrophic occurrences since it's quite improbable that you'll have tens of thousands of dollars accessible if you had some significant medical issue. The amount of additional coverage you ultimately choose to get is entirely up to you. For instance, some plans are more expensive because they include things like regular medical checkups and medicines. However, you may be able to forgo this kind of coverage if your income is sufficient to allow you to pay cash for these expenses and you don't need frequent medical visits or prescription medication. Just be certain that you are well aware of your demands before making that choice.

Property and casualty insurance, sometimes referred to as auto insurance, house insurance, renters insurance, and so on, is the second kind of coverage that is required by law in the majority of US states. Like health insurance, auto and house insurance are often required, but it's still a good idea to have them to protect against unforeseen costs of tens of thousands of dollars to replace or repair lost, damaged, or stolen property. Having a game plan is a smart idea since, even worse, if you caused a car accident, for instance, and someone's medical costs exceeded $100,000, you might be held responsible for that. Similar to health insurance, the kind of coverage depends greatly on the person receiving it and the sort of life they lead. For instance, you may accept a greater deductible if you wanted to lower your monthly cost. Alternately, if you believe that you are more irresponsible than others, you may want to choose a higher level of coverage just in case. In any event, consider your alternatives, consider who you are and how you live your life, then choose a course of action that makes sense for you.

Long-term care and disability insurance are two more types of coverage. Again, to determine whether they are appropriate for you, you really need to consider your individual circumstances. Disability insurance, for instance, may not be worthwhile if your employment isn't extremely hazardous. However, the majority of experts would advise you to check into long-term care insurance simply because it will be expensive for you to live out your days as an elderly person and someone else will have to pay for your care if you need it. Depending entirely on your decision, it may be the insurance provider or it might be you. It can be possible to live without long-term care insurance if you have enough money to meet your demands. But if you're thinking about living into your old age, this is a choice you should take carefully.

Let's quickly go through some additional liability and umbrella insurance policy options. The majority of these plans are beneficial when there is a greater chance of being sued, mostly because you have the financial resources to fight back against claims. It could be a wise choice if you are in a situation in your life where you are concerned about this and the cost of these sorts of insurances makes sense. Analyze your predicament to determine whether or not you need this kind of protection.

Life insurance is the last sort of insurance we'll discuss. I've put this for last because there are some competing theories about the kind of life insurance you need to get, and it's time to include you in the discussion rather than having it without you. There are two fundamental forms of life insurance, and each has variants and add-ons. Most of them are considered to be wastes of money since they effectively involve wagering on factors like as how you'll die and whether you'll become crippled before that. Whole life insurance is the first category. This is a life insurance policy that protects you in the case of your death and includes a portion for time savings and investment. You might discover alternative ways to invest this money at a higher rate of return if the rate of return on the savings portion of these products is generally not outstanding. Additionally, these plans are substantially more expensive.

Term life insurance is an option to whole life insurance. These are contracts with a set duration, often up to 30 years. You and your family won't be compensated if you pass away after the term has ended. Furthermore, these insurance don't have a savings or investment component that may be used to accumulate funds over time. as, compared to whole life insurance, these plans are sometimes far more affordable, giving you the freedom to invest your money as you see right.

Here is the contradictory idea that financial "gurus" and advisers both share. Advisors would advise you that purchasing whole life insurance has additional advantages since you are protected till death, regardless of when you pass away, and you have access to an integrated savings plan. Gurus would advise you to acquire term life insurance and invest your savings instead of wasting your money on such a subpar savings strategy. Both of these proposals have the drawback of not taking you into account. For instance, what did you do with $200 you got last time that wasn't designated to pay any bills, simply additional cash? If you're like the majority of individuals, you just spent money on items you want, such as dining out, additional clothing, or whatever. If you fit this description, which describes the majority of Americans, you probably shouldn't buy term insurance and invest the remaining funds because you'll probably spend the money anyway, and a 0% return on your investment is always worse than the savings plan that a whole life policy can provide. However, if you have the discipline to invest your savings and get term insurance, that's definitely the best course of action for you because your money would most likely have higher returns. The best approach for you will emerge once you examine your spending patterns and are honest with yourself.

Amount In Pocket

You may establish the budget available for a certain category by keeping the money in your pocket. Cash rather than plastic money is meant by the term "money" in this context. Although plastic money, such as debit and credit cards, offer advantages of their own, they are also a source of revenue destruction. It prevents someone from calculating how much money they have spent. It is advised to carry hard cash or a debit card from a different spending account while going food shopping in order to be recognized as a savvy spender. If you have money, you may limit your purchases to requirements and stick to one single item. Your ability to follow your budget is limited by the money you have in your pocket. It stops you from overspending on a desire. Shopping with cash in hand is preferable than using a card or other plastic money, which might give you a heart attack when you see the bill at the end of each month.

Cash implies the seller has immediate access to the funds to cover ongoing company expenses. Cash poses a risk of theft and is a less secure form of payment since it cannot be stopped, while a card may be blocked or traced if it is lost, stolen, or used covertly.

while taking into account the use of plastic money. They are more convenient and secure than cash, but they also encourage overspending and uncontrollable budgets. As was already indicated, financial institutions also levy a number of hidden fees for these services. However, one requires a functioning bank account in order to access plastic money. You may get a ton of offers, discounts, and bargains with plastic money, especially a credit card, as most banking channels have agreements with the owners of fast food franchises, restaurants, and shopping malls to supply these services. Although you may first find these conveniences to be appealing and a source of delight, you will eventually realize that the majority of the items you purchased in a hurry out of a desire for presents and discounts are useless to you and that you wasted the money you had set aside for a necessary purchase. Some store owners may give you discounts if you pay them in cash. Find such stores to fulfill your long-term needs, and it is true that buying with cash helps you be able to save money better than paying with a card or cash, and that cash is a useful tool for helping you keep better tabs on your spending.

The majority of the time, American shoppers don't want to pay with cash. Only 26% of the respondents' total purchases, according to a poll of 3,016 Americans, were done using cash. They said they prefer to pay in cash for all transactions under $10 and try using a credit card or debit card after that. Almost 30% of the transactions used debit cards. According to the statistics, Americans who make a high salary and are older than 60 have more cash on hand than Americans who are younger or from other socioeconomic classes.

Share Payment by Instrument Use (Cash, Debit Cards, Credit Cards, etc.) is shown in Figure 9.

Because there is a larger likelihood of theft and robbery, the majority of Americans do not carry cash. They avoid carrying cash and choose plastic money over cash for the same reason. According to the FBR, the following percentages of thefts and crimes involving cash occurred in 2017:

Figure 10: Cash Robberies in the US in 2017

AVOID DOOR SHOPPING

From the windows, the idea of window shopping was born. Most physical businesses have a glass window where the merchants exhibit a vibrant display to get clients in. This time-honored method of marketing succeeded in drawing in a sizable client base. The typical buyer only looks at a display for eleven seconds, thus merchants and store owners need to be inventive when designing their displays. Women are said to be polychronic, and Varsha Jain notes that women tend to acquire more clothing, accessories, and other adornments. Your money, investments, and income are all threatened by window shopping. The majority of experts advise against doing so since they believe it wastes your time, effort, and money. Instead, go for a stroll in a local park or watch a movie. It eats away at your money. Window shopping is nothing more than visiting the mall and perusing the displays, and for the same reasons, advertisers employ vibrant displays to draw your attention and inspire you to switch your attention from window shopping to real purchasing. Window shopping, however, offers benefits while seeming to have a lot of drawbacks. If a person is able to manage the impulse to really buy anything, he or she may discover cost-effective locations to get everyday necessities at a lower cost than the normal shopping locations.

According to a statistic, women are more likely than males to do window shopping. According to a New York daily news source, a woman spends about 400 hours and makes 301 visits to the supermarket on average each year. According to The Real Cost of Your Shopping Habits (2015), out of 400 hours, 190 hours are spent shopping for clothing, shoes, or window shopping. Americans are thoughtless consumers; whether we go shopping online or in person, we should remember that we are only here to purchase products that are required and should resist from purchasing additional items that are either expensive or worthless. As a result, it is advised that someone who wishes to save money spend less on shopping. Window shopping may be done physically or online, as was already established, but both have comparable effects. Both put financial strain on the customers' well-being. In reality, marketers make a lot of effort to alter customer perceptions and transform visitors' intentions from window shopping to actual purchase.

Window shopping online is no different. Imagine you are browsing through your mobile phone and an advertising appears. Usually, you would hit the cancel button, but what if the displayed screen included something you had been searching for a long time? It can be something you desire or something you need. The stuff you view online often comes from your search history. These commercials are produced using cookies and data that marketers have bought in order to disturb your peace of mind and persuade you to invade more. Even while online window shopping and browsing fulfill your want to shop and visit marketplaces, they lead to significant expenditure. When you purchase in-person or online, it may be challenging to maintain financial control. A shopaholic cannot resist making a purchase despite window browsing. When you promise to stick to your budget, only the sincerity of your intentions count.

Avoid using a credit card or a mobile wallet.

Money is needed to go shopping for necessities or hobbies. However, it has previously been said that using plastic money, such as debit or credit cards, for shopping is preferable. Plastic money purchases result in a never-ending debt load that requires interest and other fees. Therefore, paying with cash is preferable than using a credit card or debit card. Customers are solicited through social media to make quick and simple purchases via large companies like Amazon, Ali Baba, and Ali Express in the era of globalization. Items are often displayed in appealing shapes and sizes to draw in customers. People utilized plastic money, such as debit cards, credit cards, or mobile payments, in these purchases. A person's wallet will be burdened if they use a credit card to purchase anything since they will have to pay extra taxes and interest on the transaction. People often turn to plastic money during times of pandemic (covid - 19), since currency notes are one of the corona virus' carriers. If we look at Amazon's financial report for the 2019–2020 fiscal year, it is evident that more consumers choose to shop there than at malls.

Figure 11: Financial Chart for Amazon in 2020

Everything you purchase online is unreliable in terms of quality and quantity since companies like Amazon and Ali Baba require upfront payments, make it impossible to return items, and take a long time to reimburse customers. When paying with cash, customers are free to choose whatever item they choose, with no sacrifice on quality or quantity. Additionally, customers have the chance to research additional information and veracity. Another factor that a company owner thinks about more is reliability. As the single benefactor of his enterprise, he wants his customers to have faith in him and stick with him and his goods. Customers also want to spend their money on products that are trustworthy and guaranteed by people they can rely on, both in terms of physical and intangible goods. Such guarantees are not verified nor trustworthy in digital media since it is impossible to believe someone you have just spoken to once or whose employer is unknown. In today's high-tech society, individuals employ a variety of technologies to commit fraud against one another, with credit cards, debit cards, and mobile payments being their main targets. These con artists prey on unknowing victims who are easy prey since they lack understanding of hi-tech tools. For the next 15 days, the central bank will detain money in its vaults to cleanse it of COVID-19. The Covid-19 pandemic is being addressed, and several pharmaceutical firms are striving to create a vaccine that will eradicate this threat from the planet.

"KEEP CHANGE" in the container

Big businesses have employed a variety of financial consultants, and often they are charged with advising clients on how to reduce overhead costs and make more money, however sometimes you may hear someone discuss domestic savings. The expression "little drops of water make a mighty ocean" is often used to convey the idea that success does not come easily and requires patience and hard effort. Typically, after a shopping trip, we avoid storing change in our pockets or wallet and instead spend our pennies on strange items or ask the shopkeeper to hold onto the change. This behavior will not only cost you money, but it will also boost the sales of the merchant in question, who is already making a respectable profit from his trade.

By purchasing a cup of coffee, for instance, you may wind up with a little bit more in savings:

Coffee costs $1.43.

$0.57 was rounded up and put into savings.

$2.00 has been charged in total (deducted from your checking account).

The additional $0.57 is transferred to a connected savings account with the intention that you won't even know it left your checking account. If you make many purchases throughout the course of the day, it will add up to a few dollars in daily savings or a respectable monthly increase in your savings. Consider this to be comparable to a holiday savings account, to which you may put a little amount each day of the year with the goal of having a few additional hundred dollars saved up by the end of the month.

A fantastic example of how to save money is a child's piggybank. Parents put their spare change in these banks, and when they break it later, they may use the money to give their children thoughtful gifts or other nice things. You need to develop this habit. We realize it won't accomplish your goals, but at some point it will save you from excruciating suffering. Coin collecting is an excellent hobby since, over time, a coin may become uncommon and, if sold, may bring you a beautiful sum that you weren't expecting. People often don't carry coins in their pockets. By adopting this strategy, you can demonstrate how much money you can easily save each month and how much we can save by KEEPING CHANGE IN THE CAN. The best method to save money is to "serve yourself first." At the end of the day, you will have a nice sum of money that you can use to purchase anything you want or to spend a vacation at a lovely location with your family and friends. Banks these days provide a program wherein for each transaction you make, you will get a sizeable number of points that, after around a month, may be used to make purchases. Although this sum is really little, it serves as a means of luring customers, and the more transactions you complete, the more money or points you will get.

Consequences of Debt Non-Payment:

Americans sometimes, if not more often, are unable to pay their financial commitments. In this situation, declaring bankruptcy would seem like the wisest course of action, but what about the institution from whom the money was borrowed? In these specific cases, the system advises taking the following steps, which are outlined below:

The Collection Agency: If a debt is not being paid, the collectors will refer the account to a collection agency. According to federal law, a debt that has been unpaid for 31 days must be reported to a collection agency. However, the amount that is past due varies from 31 to 180 days. The inquiry is completed by the collecting agency in approximately a year. The lenders often pay a fee to the collection firms in the range of 25% to 45%.

When a Debt Collector Contacts You:

Following the submission of the report to the collection agency, the collection agency agents begin contacting you and sending you legal notices. Therefore, it is strongly advised to pay off the loan as quickly as feasible.

Impact negatively on credit ratings: The debt score is important. The borrower's capacity to promptly and effectively repay the loan without any delays affects the ratings. The banks and financial institutions will affect a person's financial ratings if it proved difficult for him or her to repay the obligation.

Therefore, it is advised that you avoid going down the route of piling up debt, and if for some reason you did manage to do so, attempt to get rid of it as quickly as you can.

Debt Haunting: The longer it takes for the debt to leave you, the more money it costs. It will have an impact on your financial status, and American laws are highly aggressive when someone sues you for failing to repay their money if there is a chance you may end up on the default list.

Remember that despite everything, life carries on. Therefore, it is advised to consider all options carefully, especially when it comes to debt. However, it takes between three and 10 years to become debt-free. If you learn that you borrowed money from the bank in error, don't feel bad about it; instead, focus on paying it back while you relax. Making ourselves panic will undoubtedly make things worse. Decide carefully and have a fulfilling life.

Kill That Debt

Given that you are gaining velocity every day while driving the money car, you should be in third gear right about now. Congratulations for taking charge of your finances and making some really wise financial choices. At this stage in your trip, you are beginning to accumulate some monetary reserves, and you have every right to feel proud of yourself. But let's avoid being smug. One step to gaining control over your finances is to actually start saving money. Getting it to function for you is the next step. Even while it may be great to have a few hundred or even a few thousand dollars saved up, if all it is doing is gathering dust and earning almost no interest, it isn't doing you any good to have it put away. What steps can you take then to make your money work in your favor?

First off, a little issue with something called debt is one of the things that increasingly burdens individuals. Nearly everyone has it in some capacity; it is a persistent, nagging, royal pain in the you know what. If properly leveraged, debt may be advantageous since it puts you in a better position to build wealth over time. What am I referring to here? A excellent illustration is a mortgage. You will probably have to take on the biggest and costliest debt load of your life at this point. However, if properly planned for, handled, and the best bargains are consistently acquired via remortgages, you will eventually find yourself in possession of a very solid long-term investment that should provide a healthy return. This indicates that your money is working for you rather than against you.

Debt, however, may have the opposite effect and be crippling. When credit cards and loans have high interest rates, it may get out of hand and leave you unable to make the minimal payment every month. When this happens, debt stops being good and turns into a weapon for leveraging, digging you further into a hole that you may find yourself in and may find it difficult to escape. Now that the gloom and doom has passed, what steps can you do right now to minimize and ultimately get rid of whatever bad debt you may have?

One thing you may do is use part of the funds you have carefully been saving to begin repaying the debt you have been carrying about with high interest rates. You will be better off the sooner you get rid of this. The sooner you can amass more money to put into your savings and investment account, as well as your piggy bank, the better. For one thing, you won't have an additional expense to keep paying out each month (a major tick for your budget plan). Just about how much money you might be saving up each month if you didn't have to pay that bothersome loan or credit card bill, or both!

If the only thing you take away from this chapter is the knowledge that if you have a lot of poor debt payments eating away at your money, whatever savings you make will quickly be nullified.

Naturally, you should always check to see if paying off a debt earlier than what has been agreed upon will result in any penalties, and you should always be familiar with the terms and conditions of any financial agreement you enter into both before and during the duration of the arrangement. Be aware of where you may make larger and extra payments toward the debt without incurring any penalties and make sure there are no unpleasant, hidden fees that might come back to bother you. Your debts will be paid off faster if you put more money toward them. Another short suggestion is to always pay off the loan with the highest APR or interest rate. It makes little sense to carefully pay off the personal loan with an APR of 5.9% if you also have a credit card balance of £3000 with a 17.9% interest rate. Prior to focusing on the personal loan, you must first aim and pay off the credit card as rapidly as you can.

Another strategy frequently employed by what are affectionately known as "credit card tarts" is to consider switching a debt with a high interest rate accruing debt to one with a lower APR, thereby reducing the monthly repayments necessary to clear the debt and leaving more money to pay additional amounts off of your overall debt burden. With relation to credit cards, one approach to achieve this is to attempt to move to a 0% interest program. However, it's crucial that you once again get aware with the switching costs that are sometimes included with these agreements and determine if they are a reasonable bargain for lowering your debt.

There are various choices for managing debt, and as I've previously said, I don't pretend to be an expert. If you don't feel confident doing this on your own, you should always seek credible professional counsel. If you believe your credit rating may be in doubt and you are unsure if you would be qualified to apply for a 0% credit card, for instance, you should also get a copy of your credit report.

A dictionary of important organizations that may assist you further if you need further assistance with debt management and getting your credit report is provided at the conclusion of the book.

The following is a summary of the major themes this chapter covered:

Utilize a solid debt as leverage.

Eliminate bad debt as soon as you can

First, pay off bad debt using savings.

Consider changing your choices to reduce the amount of interest you pay on your loans.

Always read the fine print to understand any penalties you may be subject to, such as if you pay off your loan before the deadline.

Always settle your debts in order of highest APR first.

Be tenacious. Never stop trying to pay off bad debt. Once you get rid of it, you'll have so much more money available, which you may put into your savings and investment account or that dreaded piggy bank!

Control Your Spending By Following Your Budget.

Budgeting is the process of developing a plan for your expenses. You must now consider your overall income before creating a budget, followed by all of your expenses. One of the most important aspects of money management is controlling your budget. When regulating your financial planning, three factors need to be taken into account.

Identify areas of your budget where you may make savings. Make an effort to distinguish between your major requirement and any supporting needs. You will be able to manage your spending if you can at least partially prove your secondary demands. For instance, if your monthly cell payment is $300, you should see whether you can cut that amount in half to $150 by adjusting your call time or restricting your use.Try to negotiate lower rates on all of your bills. Even Sky TV subscribers may get discounts if they announce their intention to depart. Give it a go; you could be pleasantly pleased.

Pay off credit cards and debts.

One of the easiest money management advices is to pay off debt. If you have a credit card and a loan, you must pay both a high rate of interest and installment payments. In these situations, it's critical to pay off debts first. You will be able to set aside the monthly payment plus interest after the loan is paid off. You'll be able to save more money if you pay off your bills. It may seem absurd, but once you are debt-free, you will have more cash on hand or in your bank account.

When going shopping, it is best to leave your credit card at home. You won't wind up overpaying thanks to it.

saving

In certain cases, controlling your fixed costs and committed expenses may result in some financial excess. You have a surplus of this amount. After setting up an emergency fund, you may search the market for worthwhile investment options or start a high-interest savings account. Here, you may either withdraw your money as required or leave it in the bank for a time to earn a nice rate of interest.

How to budget on a tight budget

Saving money while living on a low salary is definitely feasible. Here, you must retain a sharp focus on your saving objective.

If you quit dining out and bring homemade food to work for lunch, you may save a significant sum of money.

Use power wisely and attempt to get equipment that are energy efficient. Naturally, your power bill will be lower.

Use online or Sunday coupons to save money while buying groceries; these days, you may even get discounts when buying new clothing. Avoid making impulsive purchases. Instead, buy things when you can acquire them at a cheap price. Spend some time looking for what you want and spend even more time discovering the cheapest seller.

Offer handmade presents to your pals for their birthdays and other occasions; this will demonstrate your interest for them and enable you to save money on gift purchases.

Online stores and physical stores both provide a variety of super saver plans, which you may subscribe to in order to see the best deals on purchases. In the end, you will significantly reduce your costs.

Income: Invest To Increase Earnings

One of life's most important lessons is how to invest. A business degree is not necessary to understand how to invest money wisely. To develop a successful strategy, a person just requires a fundamental knowledge of business.

The Purpose of Investment

Everybody has their own financial objectives, and investing is a terrific method to achieve them. Investment requires diligent labor and careful preparation. People who just want to spend a little amount of money in the hopes that it would grow to be millions of dollars are unlikely to succeed.

To be able to pay their expenses, people need to have an investment that can provide adequate income in the form of dividends or interest. Keep in mind that these assets shouldn't be sold since they are needed to maintain the existing standard of living.

The best investments

Stocks and bonds are the two most common types of investments. Bonds are a sort of financing, while stocks are ownership in the corporation. Mutual funds allow investors to purchase stocks and bonds on their behalf.

Bonds

A bond is a security that pays its owner a regular sum on a predetermined schedule. Bonds are a kind of debt security where the issuers are the borrowers and the investors are the lenders. As a result, issuing a bond entails borrowing money from investors.

A standard bond typically pays interest based on its face value twice a year in the form of a coupon rate. The duration and the credit quality are the two elements that determine the coupon rate. Higher coupon rates are offered on longer-term bonds to make up for the risk that investors are incurring and the longer wait period before receiving income. The issuer's capacity to pay interest and principal when due is referred to as the credit quality. Bonds with lower credit ratings have higher coupon rates to offset the possibility of issuer default.

Treasury securities, corporate bonds, and municipal bonds are the three different forms of bonds. Because they are guaranteed by the federal bank, government-issued Treasury securities are among the safest options for investments. Private corporations issue corporate bonds. The degree of risk associated with these bonds varies according on how well the firm can pay.

Similar to federal bonds, municipal bonds are issued by local governments.

Stocks

Because they would reflect a portion of ownership in the firm upon purchase, stocks are often referred to as equities. Dividends and price growth are the two ways stocks may generate income.

A company's success draws investors to invest in it, which causes the price of the stock to rise as supply and demand are balanced. Appreciation is the term used to describe a price rise. When equities are sold for more than they were originally purchased for, investors might benefit. A company may pay a dividend based on the number of shares a stockholder owns each quarter. Dividends are often offered to stockholders as rewards.

Stocks come in two varieties: favored and common. The price of preferred stock fluctuates less than that of ordinary stock. This form of stock is preferred by conservative investors or those who do not wish to take on more risk. The fact that preferred stock nearly always gets dividends and is paid out ahead of regular stockholders is another benefit of preferred stock. Preferred stock's lack of voting rights prevents its investors from being involved in management decisions, which is a drawback.

Common stock investors take on more risk than preferred stock holders and may or may not get dividends, but they have the potential to reap huge rewards, making them the purest kind of stock. Common stocks are a better alternative for those looking to profit from price growth since they are less expensive and have far more frequent market movements.

Do You Want To Become A Better Money Manager? This Is How:

1You must save more and for longer periods of time if you want to earn more overtime. For instance, you may create a savings account at the bank, and at the end of each month, a set amount is transferred from your personal account to the savings account. You are not permitted to withdraw funds from such types of accounts, so you may save money that will grow over time.

2. Making your own financial plans and saving. For instance, if you began working at age 20, say, and you started saving $100 each month, by the end of the year you would have $1200 saved up, not including interest. You would have $54,000 in savings by the time you turn 65, not including interest gained on top of that or pensions or other income you would have received. Thus, you can see that saving does not necessarily have

to be substantial; it may instead be modest, but over time, every dollar adds up.

3. You must create objectives if you want to get wealthy. Setting objectives gives you a way to control your need to purchase less important items. When it comes time to draw out your strategy (money pulse), writing down your objectives will help you prioritize spending. Making a list of your financial objectives, both short- and long-term, makes decision-making simpler.

Money Management Apps.

In today's technologically advanced world, you may monitor your budget using a wide variety of software (apps). Some of the applications on the list below may be found for free in the app stores on your smartphones and tablets and are quite useful.

1. AndroMoney - This expenditure tracker and money management software has a built-in calculator, numerous accounts, support for cloud storage, synchronization with other devices, and password security. It also supports multiple accounts. For those who don't need anything substantial, it's a straightforward, reliable introduction.

2. Bitcoin Wallet provides a number of Bitcoin-inspired features, such as the ability to purchase more Bitcoin, pay for items using Bitcoin, and access

management tools including transaction history, balance, and transaction specifics. If your phone is stolen, you may even remotely deactivate access to it.

3. Another straightforward tool that might help you manage your money is Cash. There are no ads. Additionally, you may export in CSV, get summary reports, backup to Dropbox, and use it in any of four languages. To further assist you in understanding how you are spending your money, it also includes a number of charts.

www.ingramcontent.com/pod-product-compliance
Lightning Source LLC
Chambersburg PA
CBHW050236120526
44590CB00016B/2106